VINTAGE WARBIRDS No 5

Cover illustration: N5350 was the first Sopwith triplane to be built by Clayton & Shuttleworth Ltd. It was at Eastchurch on 20 December 1916, when it was flown by Sqn. Cdr. Harry Busteed, and remained there at least until 13 February 1917. It subsequently saw operational use with No. 10 (Naval) Sqn., and was deleted on 24 October 1917.

1. Sopwith Dolphins equipped No. 1 Sqn. Canadian Air Force (No. 81 Sqn. (Canadian), RAF) from its formation on 20 November 1918 until April 1919. This line-up of some of its aircraft, presumably at Upper Heyford, includes E4764, F7085, F7076, J3, J15 and E4776; all bear the maple-leaf device adopted by the squadron as its marking. (Public Archives Canada)

Vintage Warbirds No 5

THE Sopwith FIGHTERS

J. M. BRUCE

ARMS AND ARMOUR PRESS

Published in 1986 by Arms & Armour Press Ltd.,
2–6 Hampstead High Street, London NW3 1QQ.

Distributed in the United States by Sterling Publishing Co. Inc., 2 Park Avenue, New York, N.Y.10016.

© Arms & Armour Press Ltd., 1986
All rights reserved. No part of this publication may be reproduced, stored in a retrieval system, or transmitted in any form by any means electrical, mechanical or otherwise, without first seeking the written permission of the copyright owner.

British Library Cataloguing in Publication Data:
Bruce, J. M.
The Sopwith fighters.—(Vintage warbirds illustrated; v. 5)
1. Great Britain. *Royal Air Force* 2. Camel (Fighter planes) 3. European War, 1914-1918—Aerial operations, British
I. Title II. Series
940.4′4941   D602

ISBN 0-85368-790-0

Editing, design and artwork by Roger Chesneau.
Typesetting by Typesetters (Birmingham) Ltd.
Printed and bound in Italy
by GEA/GEP in association with
Keats European Ltd., London.

◀2
2. Both the Royal Flying Corps (RFC) and the Royal Naval Air Service (RNAS) experimented with overwing mountings for a forward-firing Lewis gun on their Sopwith Pups, but these efforts were not wholly successful. Here Flight Sub-Lieutenant (FSL) W. H. Chisam stands beside a two-gun Pup of No. 3 (Naval) Sqn. (E. Pierce)

Introduction

Those who are well instructed in the history of the military aviation of the 1914–18 war readily associate the names of certain aircraft manufacturers with fighting aeroplanes – that is, with aircraft having as their primary function the pursuit and destruction in combat of their adversaries. In France the names of Nieuport and the SPAD, in Germany Albatros, Pfalz and Fokker, and in Britain Bristol and Sopwith, evoke memories of distinguished fighting aeroplanes and the young men who flew them in this newest aspect of warfare.

The Sopwith Aviation Co. Ltd. had, perhaps more than most of its wartime contemporaries, something of history on its side. The high-speed single-seat scouting aircraft that was the progenitor of the armed fighter was a British concept, first expressed in the elegant little BS1 (soon renamed SE2) created at the Royal Aircraft Factory, Farnborough, in 1912–13 by Geoffrey de Havilland. But the first such aircraft to be built in quantity against a military order was the Sopwith SS1 Tabloid, a slightly modified development of the (very) sporting two-seater of November 1913 – yet its only significant feat of arms was an early bombing raid on the airship sheds at Düsseldorf.

Many of the long line of Sopwith single-seat fighters reflected the general proportions and configuration of the Tabloid. Handling qualities, as judged by the relatively naïve standards of the time, varied markedly, but most Sopwith fighters were well liked by most of their pilots. With their two-seat fighters the Sopwith company enjoyed less success – the early gun-carrying pushers did no fighting as such – but the 1½-Strutter remains a classic and historic type.

From the endearing Pup, engaging triplane and electrifying Camel of 1916 to the enigmatic Snapper and Snark of 1918–19 may have seemed like rapid and substantial progress at the time, and by the standards of the period considerable advances were made. Yet the all-seeing and omniscient eye of hindsight may now discern a logical and straightforward line of airframe development unaccompanied operationally by any significant improvement in weight of fire, save only in the Dolphin (which had its supplementary armament halved by official decree) and perhaps in the Snark (which was too late to be considered and may not even have flown with its optimistic six-gun armament). And the last Sopwith fighter designs were doomed, through no fault of their own, by their incurably defective ABC Wasp and Dragonfly engines.

What is remarkable is how so much design, development and production effort was compressed into a mere five years. One can reflect sadly that almost all of it happened because the world was at war; yet realism urges recognition of thankfulness that the Sopwith fighters and their contemporaries managed, with the odds against them, to do their martial job so well. They should not be forgotten, nor should the men who created and flew to war in them.

A substantial number of the photographs used in this book came from the friends to whom they are credited, and to whom I am greatly indebted for their use. Those attributed to Peter Liddle are from his 1914–18 Personal Experience Archives presently housed within Sunderland Polytechnic. As always, my greatest indebtedness is to Stuart Leslie, who over many years has done so much to secure the preservation of historic photographs and has always aided me without stint.

J. M. Bruce

▲3

3. The earliest gun-carrying Sopwiths were pusher seaplanes of at least three types. Five ordered by Greece were impressed for the RNAS on the outbreak of war, and at least three (897, 900 and 901) were converted to landplanes. These had the 100hp Gnome Monosoupape, and 901 was flown to Eastchurch via Hendon as a landplane on 25 and 26 September 1914. The aircraft illustrated was probably one of the three.

▼4

4. Six Sopwith-built gun-carrying landplanes (801–806) were supplied to the RNAS from October 1914. The first two were reported to have 110hp Sunbeams, the remainder 150hp Sunbeam Crusaders. No. 805 was preparing for trials at Brooklands on 12 March 1915, was at Hendon (the locale of this photograph) on 17 April 1915, went to Chingford on 13 July, and was dismantled there on 16 August 1915.

5. While at Hendon No. 805 was fitted with a bomb sight, and subsequent Sunbeam-powered Sopwith Gun Buses had provision for bomb racks. Thirty (3833–3862) were ordered from Robey & Co. Here seen at Lincoln racecourse for tests by Harry Hawker (second from left), 3833 arrived at RNAS Detling on 10 February 1916 for use as a bombing trainer but, together with 3835, 3838 and 3841, was badly damaged by a gale on 16 February. By January 1917 only one remained in commission.

6. First of the long line of Sopwith single-engine tractor single-seat scouts and fighters was the SS1 Tabloid, of which twelve were ordered for the Military Wing of the RFC in December 1913 and March 1914. The first production Tabloid appeared at Brooklands on 11 April 1914 and was delivered to Farnborough on 22 April. Here, 326 is seen at Farnborough in a photograph dated 23 May 1914. Four SS1s were sent to France on 18 August, and one of these (387) was flown as a fighter by Norman Spratt several times late in August, armed with only a revolver.

▲7

▲8 ▼9

7. Two of the RFC's SS1 Tabloids, plus the prototype, were transferred to the RNAS in September 1914, but the twelve production Tabloids (1201–1212) delivered against the Navy's own contract were SS2s. These had ailerons, zero stagger, 'V'-strut undercarriages and larger tailplanes. The first six went to the Aegean in HMS *Ark Royal* and saw limited service with Nos. 2 and 3 Wings RNAS. Here 1205, with overwing Lewis gun, is seen on Imbros. This SS2 was in course of return from the Aegean on 1 October 1915.

8. Whatever No. 1213 was, it was not contractually related to 1210–1212, for it was delivered to Hendon as early as 10 November 1914 and had an 80hp Le Rhône. This photograph is of 1214, delivered to Hendon on 19 November 1914; it may have been intended as a second-string Gordon Bennett entrant to the more radical 1215. No. 1214 went to Dover on 4 April 1915, thence to No. 1 (Naval) Wing, Dunkerque, where it had the Morane-Saulnier deflector propeller and fixed Lewis gun seen here.

9. Some impression of No. 1214 may be gained from this enlargement of a small area of the background in a photograph that has as its primary subject the Morane-Saulnier Type L No. 3253 on which FSL R. A. W. Warneford fought the action of 7 June 1915 for which he was awarded the Victoria Cross. The place is, of course, Dunkerque. No. 1214 was later recorded at Dover on 16 February 1916.

10. A floatplane conversion of the Tabloid with the 100hp Gnome Monosoupape won the Schneider contest of 1914 in spectacular fashion. This variant was ordered in quantity for the RNAS and was known as the Sopwith Schneider. No. 3726 here exemplifies the small fin, warping wings, bullnose cowling and Lewis gun installation of the early Schneider. Delivered to Calshot by Harry Hawker on 23 August 1915, it was completely wrecked the next day; its pilot, FSL John MacLarty, was killed.

11. This photograph of Schneider No. 3804 at the Isle of Grain bears the date 13 March 1917. Ailerons have replaced the warping wings of the earliest production Schneider, and a larger fin has replaced the original triangular surface. No. 3804 is known to have been at RNAS Westgate in August 1917.

10▲ 11▼

▲12 ▼13

12. In later production Schneiders, the 110hp Clerget 9Z replaced the Monosoupape, and its open-front cowling changed the frontal aspect. In this form the type was usually known as the Sopwith Baby, and many were built by the Blackburn Aeroplane & Motor Co. Ltd. Here the first production Blackburn-built Baby, N1010, is seen at Grain in early December 1916, with two 65lb bombs under the fuselage. It was at RNAS Killingholme in January 1918.

13. A close-up of the Lewis gun installation and cockpit of Baby No. 8168 at Grain, 20 October 1916. This Baby was delivered to Grain by road on 28 January 1916 and its acceptance tests were flown there by Harry Hawker. It was on the strength of the Nore Flight in April 1916, is known to have been at Grain in November 1916, and was still in service at Westgate in January 1918.

14. The centre-section installation of the Lewis gun did not make for accurate shooting, and some Babies had more sensibly aligned guns. This photograph of 8151 at the Isle of Grain in June 1916 shows a Lewis gun mounted to starboard of centre; probably a Scarff synchronizing mechanism was used. This Baby was at Grain awaiting test on 21 December 1915, was tested by Hawker on 6 January 1916 and, like 8168, was on the strength of the Nore Flight in April.

15. On 8165 a Lewis gun with line-of-flight alignment was mounted centrally on the forward top decking; this aircraft also had, when photographed, a bomb rack under the fuselage. It was completed in January 1916 and was reported as serviceable at RNAS Felixstowe on 16 February.

14▲ 15▼

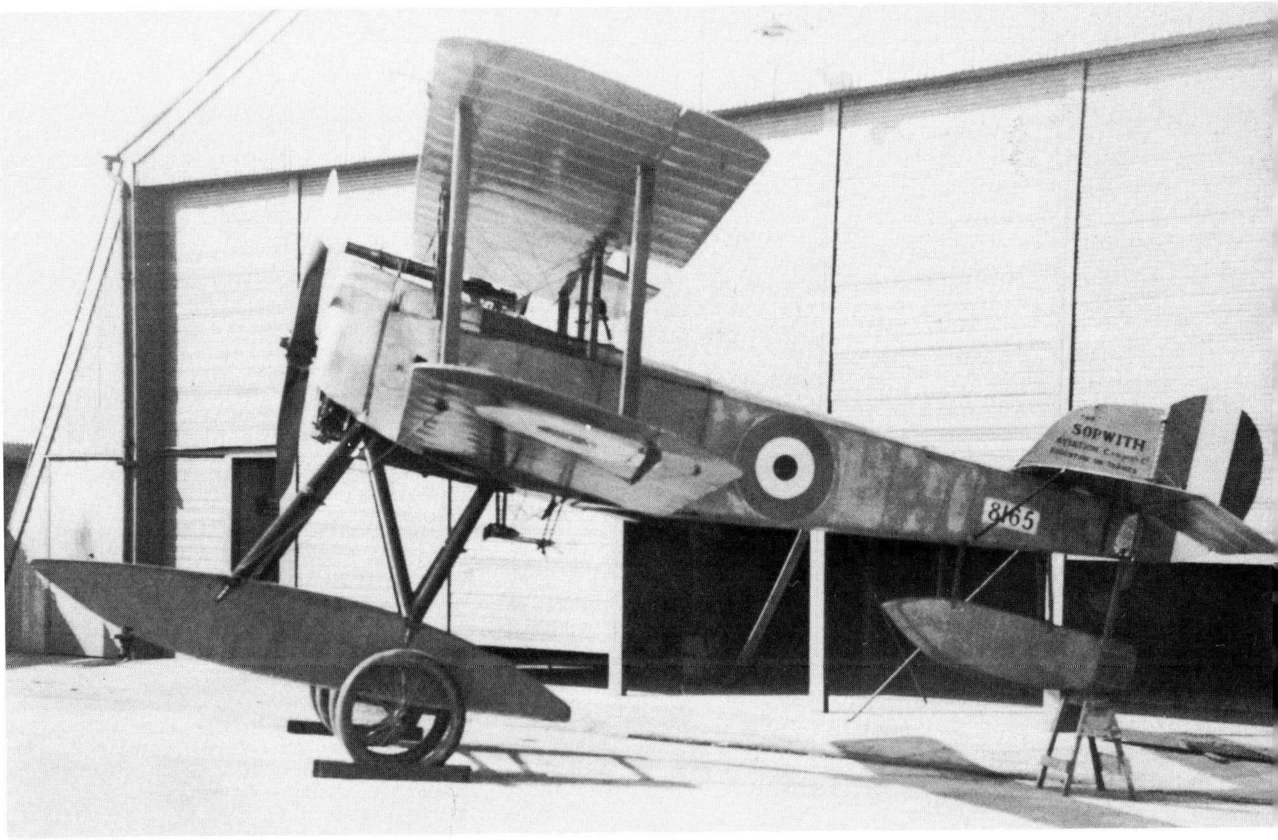

▲16

16. Yet another of the Babies of the Nore Flight in April 1916 was 8160, which had this somewhat eccentric installation of an upward-firing Lewis gun. Its acceptance test flights had been made by Harry Hawker at Grain on 7 January 1916; it was at Grain in March and June 1917, and it was still in service at Westgate on 5 January 1918. How long it retained this quaint weapon installation is not known.

17. Several Babies were given overwing installations of two side-by-side Lewis guns, but N2071 had a fixed and presumably synchronized Lewis gun on the fuselage and a second Lewis in the centre section. A 65lb bomb hangs under the fuselage. This Blackburn-built Baby had the 130hp Clerget 9B engine, and was at RNAS Killingholme on 11 January 1918.

▼17

18. The Royal Navy regarded German airships as a serious threat, and sustained experimentation with such anti-airship weapons as the Ranken explosive dart, the Davis recoilless gun and the Le Prieur rocket took place. Ranken Darts were specified as the primary armament of one batch of Blackburn-built Sopwith Babies, and at least one Baby was fitted with Le Prieur launchers for rocket missiles. This aircraft is here seen at the Isle of Grain.

19. Four Schneiders (3707, 3709, 3765 and 3806) and four Babies (8125, 8197, 8204 and 8209) were transferred to Canada. Of these, 3765 and 8209 went to the US Navy to become respectively A394 and A407 in that service, which subsequently allocated A869–872 for four Sopwith seaplanes. Here 8209, with incorrect 'N' prefix but 'A407' on its rudder, stands with a Thomas-Morse S-5, A758, in a photograph dated 6 May 1918. (US National Archives)

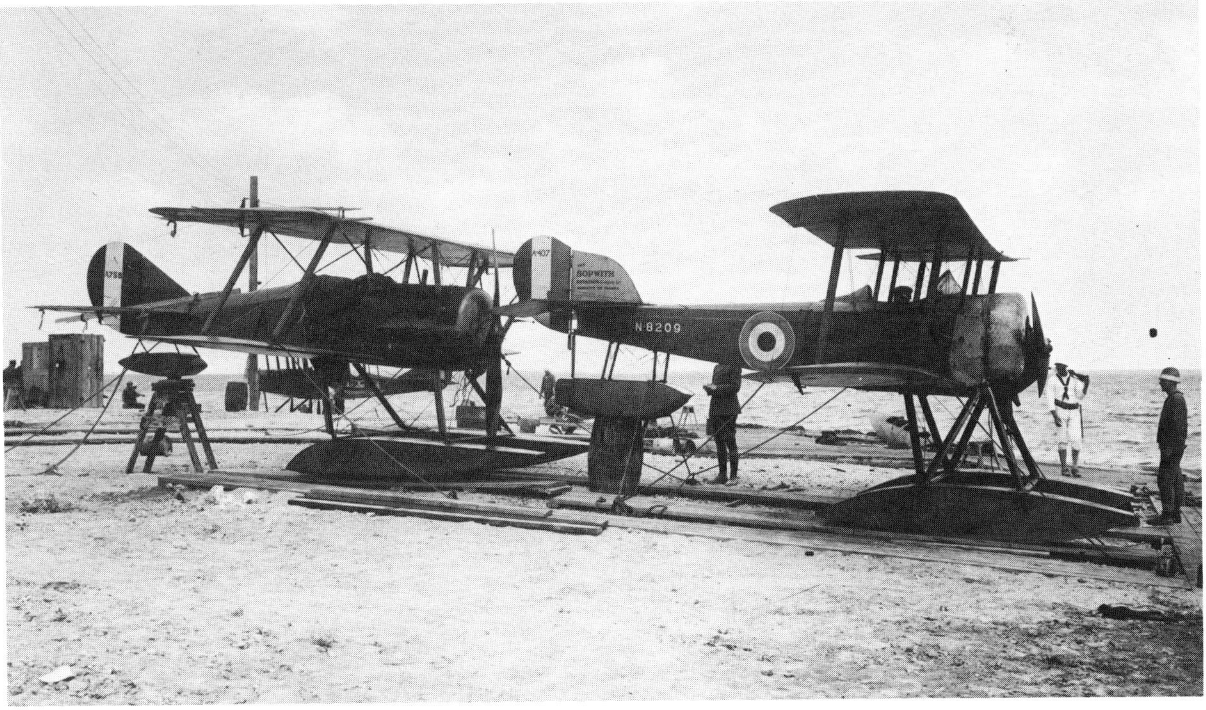

▲20

20. It seems possible that the only armament originally envisaged for the Sopwith 1½-Strutter was the observer's barbette-mounted Lewis gun, and the earliest production aircraft had no forward-firing weapon. No. 9376, the first production 1½-Strutter, saw long service with No. 5 (Naval) Wing, Dunkerque, initially with an Etévé mounting for the Lewis; later a fixed overwing Lewis was added, and when 9376 was interned in Holland on 22 April 1917 it had a fixed, synchronized Vickers and a Scarff No. 2 ring mounting. In Dutch service it became LA-42 and S412.

21. When properly armed with synchronized Vickers and Scarff-mounted Lewis guns the 1½-Strutter had a good claim to be the first true two-seat fighter. Thus armed, 9708 was photographed at Eastchurch, where it was tested by Sqn. Cdr. Harry Busteed on 11 September 1916. In common with all but a few of the early 1½-Strutters, it had the 110hp Clerget 9Z. In February 1917 it was with No. 3 Wing, RNAS.

22. The Admiralty came generously to the assistance of the RFC in the months preceding the Battle of the Somme, agreeing to transfer substantial numbers of RNAS 1½-Strutters. This enabled No. 70 Sqn. RFC to be formed on 22 April 1916. The Sopwiths of 'C' Flight, seen here, came with Scarff-Dibvosky interrupter gears and Scarff ring mountings, which greatly impressed the RFC when 'C' Flight arrived in France on 30 July 1916.

23. The earliest 1½-Strutters produced for the RFC had the Etévé gun mounting on the rear cockpit, as seen on 7777 in this photograph. Deliveries from this batch (7762–7811) built by Ruston, Proctor & Co., began in July 1916; No. 7777 went to France and was at No. 1 Aircraft Depot, (AD), St.-Omer, on 12 October 1916.

24. The 1½-Strutter was used on Home Defence duties by RFC Squadrons Nos. 37, 39, 44 and 78. A8778, built by Vickers at Crayford, was on the strength of No. 78 Sqn. at the end of October 1917, and when photographed had navigation lights and Holt flare brackets. Its national and squadron markings retained their standard coloration.

▼21

22 ▲

23 ▲   24 ▼

▲25

25. In No. 78 (HD) Sqn. some 1½-Strutters were converted into single-seaters, as exemplified by B762 which, when tested at Martlesham Heath, was armed with twin upward-firing Lewis guns. This aircraft was a Southern Aircraft Repair Depot (SARD) rebuild and was initially allocated to the RFC with the Expeditionary Force in France on 4 August 1917; a revised allocation to the Home Defence Group was made on 18 August. (E. F. Cheesman)

26. Another of No. 78 (HD) Sqn's so-called Sopwith 'Comic' single-seat conversions was A6906, but it retained the fixed Vickers gun in the normal position. The adoption of more accessibly mounted Lewis guns was virtually inevitable: no jam or other fault in the distant Vickers could be remedied in flight. A6906 had originally been ordered as a single-seat bomber from Hooper & Co. and would have had its cockpit in the standard position.

27. More 1½-Strutters were built in France than in Britain. The first examples in French service were some of the 76 transferred from the RNAS, plus six supplied direct by the Sopwith company. No. 2 of the Sopwith-built half-dozen is seen here; like early production 1½-Strutters, it lacks a Vickers gun but has an Étévé ring mounting on the rear cockpit.

28. This French 1½-Strutter had an overwing Lewis gun as forward-firing armament. The large supplementary exhaust outlet in the flank panel just behind the engine cowling was a feature of many French 1½-Strutters. (R. L. Cavanagh)

▼26

27▲ 28▼

▲29

29. A French-built 1½-Strutter of *Escadrille SOP 55* early in 1918. When a Vickers gun was installed on French-built Sopwiths it was *désaxée* slightly to port of centre, as on the Nieuports 23, 24 and 27. This aircraft has a 130hp Clerget engine, a wind-driven generator on the rear cabane struts, and a trailing aerial. (Jean Devaux)

30. The prototype Pup, developed from the little 50hp single-seater built for Harry Hawker in 1915, was completed early in February 1916. It was the first Sopwith to be specifically designed as a single-seat fighter. Tested at the Central Flying School (CFS) late in March 1916, it joined 'A' Sqn., No. 5 Wing, RNAS, at Dunkerque on 28 May 1916. Here seen at Dunkerque, it was numbered 3691, survived long operational service, and was selected for unrealized preservation in September 1918. (E. F. Cheeseman)

▼30

31. The basic armament of the Pup was a single machine gun, on most aircraft a central-fixed Vickers, as seen here (but with the Sopwith windscreen removed) on N6183 of No. 3 (Naval) Sqn. This Pup was in 'B' Flight of that unit on 12 July 1917. It was wrecked on 14 August and was at Dunkerque Depot two days later; its deletion was approved on 21 August 1917. It is believed that N6183 was also with No. 11 (Naval) Sqn. at one time. (K. M. Molson)

32. On many RNAS Pups the standard gun installation was a tripod-mounted Lewis firing at an upward angle through a cut-out in the centre section. Doubtless this was expected to facilitate attacks on enemy airships, and Pups carried on gun-turret platforms on battleships and cruisers were armed in this way. This one was photographed at RNAS Great Yarmouth. (Peter Liddle)

▲33

33. The inadequacy of the single mechanically synchronized Vickers gun was the Pup's major shortcoming, and various attempts were made by both the RNAS and RFC to augment the armament. This Beardmore-built Pup of 'C' Sqn, RNAS Imbros, sensibly combined the tripod-mounted Lewis and the normal fixed Vickers.
34. As with the Sopwith Baby, anti-airship capability demanded the arming of Pups with rockets. N5186 is seen at Eastchurch on 25 October 1916 with eight rocket tubes, apparently supplementing its Vickers gun. With pyrotechnics discarded, the aircraft was at Dunkerque by 2 November 1916, and a week later it was with the unit that became No. 8 (Naval) Sqn. It subsequently served with Nos. 3 and 4 (Naval) Sqns., crashed on 10 April and was deleted on 28 April 1917.
▼34

35. Some twenty Beardmore-built Pups had a Le Prieur rocket installation as an alternative to the Vickers gun. The standard fit was four tubes each side, but in this photograph 9926 is being hoisted aboard HMS *Vindex* with only one rocket tube either side. This Pup passed its acceptance tests on 26 February 1917 and was delivered to Felixstowe for *Vindex* on 18 March 1917.
36. B1727 was built by the Standard Motor Co. and was at SARD, Farnborough, on 10 May 1917, allocated to the Expeditionary Force. On 24 June 1917 it was issued to No. 46 Sqn. RFC, from No. 2 AD, Candas, and was among the squadron's Pups that flew to England on 10 July for Home Defence duties. Flown by 2nd Lt. N. H. Dimmock, it was one of the many aircraft that rose to attack the Gothas that bombed Southend on 12 August 1917.

35▲ 36▼

21

▲37

▲38 ▼39

37. Pups were used, relatively briefly, by Home Defence squadrons in 1917; in the hope of improving their climbing ability these aircraft had the 100hp Gnome Monosoupape engine with a characteristic cowling that had its lower segment cut away. One such was B5904 of No. 61 (HD) Sqn.

38. The ultimate expedient to enhance the Pup's performance was the fitting, in only a few aircraft, of the 110hp Le Rhône. In B5259, here photographed at London Colney, this engine had a makeshift cowling, and the armament was an overwing Lewis. Initially allocated to the Training Division, B5259 was re-assigned to the Expeditionary Force on 9 November 1917, possibly in ignorance of the decision of 6 November to abandon the Le Rhône installation. (RAF Museum)

39. Whether the Sopwith Bee, with its wing-warping lateral control, should be regarded as a fighter is debatable. It has been reported that a Vickers gun was installed in this tiny airframe, but details of where and how this was done are lacking. Used by Hawker as a personal transport, it incorporated some (probably minor) Pup components, and when photographed at Brooklands had a 50hp Gnome rotary engine.

40. The Bee was later fitted with a 30hp ABC Gnat engine, a change that may have inspired the aircraft's other name, Tadpole. Although this accentuated the aircraft's comparability to the Port Victoria PV7 and PV8, it virtually destroyed the Bee's credibility as a potential fighter. The form of the Gnat installation suggests that it may have been associated with the development of the Gnat-powered radio-controlled version of the Sopwith Sparrow. (John McCormack)

41. In its configuration the Sopwith triplane was for its time a startling departure from convention, but its rate of climb was spectacular and the pilot's view better than that of the Pup. The first prototype, N500, fitted with a 110hp Clerget, is here seen at RNAS Chingford shortly before going to 'A' Sqn, RNAS, at Furnes. It arrived there before 21 June 1916, and was finally deleted on 17 December 1917.

42. One of the most successful triplane pilots was Flt. Lt. Robert Little of No. 8 (Naval) Sqn., and N5493 was the aircraft that he flew in many combats between 28 April and 10 July 1917. It later went to No. 1 (Naval) Sqn. but was wrecked on 17 September and was finally deleted on 24 October 1917.

▲43

43. Only one Sopwith triplane, N5431, went to No. 2 Wing RNAS, in the Aegean. It was there in March 1917 and, with four 1½-Strutters, was assigned to 'E' Squadron RNAS, which was to operate from Hadzi Junas as defence against the bombers of *Kampfgeschwader I*.

44. N5431 was frequently flown by Flt. Lt. J. W. Alcock, but on 26 March 1917 it encountered a ditch during its landing run at Salonika, overturned, and was extensively damaged. (Peter Liddle)

45. After the crash of 26 March 1917, N5431 was rebuilt, perhaps with a fin of local creation; alternatively, in the course of repair, the original fin may have acquired the straight leading edge seen here. Alcock used some triplane components in a single-seat fighter of his own design, which he called his Sopwith Mouse, and later piloted the historic Vickers Vimy that made the first non-stop transatlantic flight on 14–15 June 1919. (Peter Liddle)

46. The need for heavier armament was felt by pilots of both Pups and triplanes. This triplane, thought to be No. 2 Wing's N5431, had a somewhat unpromising installation of a Lewis gun to supplement the Vickers.

▼44

45▲ 46▼

▲47

47. A few triplanes had twin Vickers guns. In the case of N5445, here photographed at Brooklands, the installation bore some resemblance to that of the Camel, the breech mechanisms of the guns being partly enclosed in a hump-like fairing. N5445 was with No. 1 (Naval) Sqn. for a time, perhaps only as a single-gun aircraft. On 29 December 1917 it was at the Experimental Armament Department, Isle of Grain. (RAF Museum)

48. Clayton & Shuttleworth built six twin-Vickers triplanes, N533–538, some of which were used by Naval Sqns. Nos. 1, 10 and 12; this twin-gun triplane at Dunkerque may have been one of them. Not surprisingly, the guns are more exposed than those on N5445 – the vital need for access to clear jams could be frustrated by enclosed installations.

▼48

49. Several RNAS triplanes were transferred to the French government, and the Sopwith company apparently built at least ten specifically for France. These equipped a French naval fighter *escadrille* at St. Pol, with which they were in service by July 1917; seven Sopwith triplanes were still on the *escadrille*'s strength on 28 February 1918. (Les Rogers)

50. Two somewhat different triplanes that owed some design features to the 1½-Strutter were built with Hispano-Suiza engines. The first, N509, had the 150hp direct-drive engine, and is here seen at Eastchurch, where it was stationed between 21 November 1916 and 2 January 1917. From Manston, May–July 1917, it flew several home-defence sorties, and was deleted there on 29 October 1917. (Harald Penrose)

▲51 ▼52

51. The second Hispano-Suiza triplane, N510, had the 200hp geared engine but was tragically short-lived. While being flown on performance tests at Eastchurch on 20 October 1916, tail flutter caused the tail unit to break away; the pilot, Flt. Lt. L. H. Hardstaff, was killed.
52. The extraordinary LRTTr three-seat triplane could have been either an escort fighter or a Home Defence aircraft possibly specializing as an anti-airship fighter. The upper gunner's nacelle, perilously placed in the top centre section, originally had the form seen in this photograph, but it was later redesigned and repositioned. Construction of the LRTTr, which had a 250hp Rolls-Royce engine, was contemporary with that of the first Clerget-powered triplane, N500.
53. An early appearance at Brooklands of the LRTTr, fully assembled with revised gunner's nacelle but before painting with PC10 finish. (Mrs Helena Lloyd, via Charles Schaedel)

54. Although the LRTTr appears to have been intended to meet the same operational requirement as the Vickers FB11, it was not allotted either an official contract or a serial number, whereas the FB11 had both. Here the completed LRTTr is seen at Brooklands with a revised and repositioned gunner's nacelle. It was an astonishingly clumsy and inept design and was quickly abandoned. (Mrs Helena Lloyd, via Charles Schaedel)

55. On the first prototype F1 Camel the upper wing was made in one piece and had no central cut-out; the engine was a 110hp Clerget 9Z, and the hump over the twin Vickers guns sloped upwards to the cockpit. The aircraft was passed by the Sopwith experimental department on 22 December 1916.

56. One of the Camel prototypes had tapered wings with 'I'-form interplane struts, and is here seen at Brooklands. Its upper wing consisted of a wide-span centre section and tapered outer panels, and there was a central cut-out in the centre section. The hump decking over the gun breeches was similar to that of production Camels, but the fairings on the undercarriage were of broad chord. (RAF Museum)

57. The tapered-wing Camel at Martlesham Heath, where it was tested in May 1917. In the test report it was recorded, somewhat improbably, as the Sopwith F1/1. Its performance was no better than that of the F1/3 with the same 130hp Clerget 9B engine; consequently the tapered-wing Camel was not considered for production.

56▲ 57▼

31

▲58

▲59 ▼60

58. The F1/3 was probably the production prototype Camel. It arrived at Martlesham Heath for official trials on 24 March 1917, and was there until early August. It returned early in January 1918 with a 110hp Le Rhône and with the positions of pilot and fuel tank transposed (effectively the prototype Home Defence conversion), was numbered B381, was at Orfordness by 27 May 1918, and flew there extensively until 3 February 1919.

59. First deliveries of production F1 Camels were made to the RNAS from May 1917. The RFC was also quick to order the type, and a sample aircraft was flown at No. 1 AD, St.-Omer, by RFC pilots on 2 and 4 March 1917. N6332 was transferred to the RFC on 25 May and is seen here at No. 2 AD, Candas, on 26 May. It went to No. 70 Sqn. RFC on 28 June but was shot down and lost on 17 July.

60. Capt. A. R. Brown, No. 209 Sqn. RAF, beside F1 Camel B7270 (150hp Bentley BR1). His most famous combat on this aircraft was that of 21 April 1918, when the two Flights that he was leading engaged a larger formation of *Jagdgeschwader 1*, led by Rittmeister Manfred, Freiherr von Richthofen. In the action von Richthofen's Fokker DrI was shot down and he was killed. (Canadian Forces)

61. Before No. 10 Sqn. RNAS lost its naval identity on the formation of the Royal Air Force its Camels bore distinctively conspicuous markings. Here is B6449, a Clerget Camel that was with No. 10 (Naval) in late January 1918. By 7 February it was with 'C' Flight of No. 9 (Naval) Sqn., but it crashed on 10 March and was deleted on 18 March 1918. (RAF Museum)

62. Although only delivered by Ruston & Hornsby (formerly Ruston Proctor) in the third week of October 1918, F3991 went to France and to No. 65 Sqn. RAF, in whose markings it is seen here. In the cockpit is Lt. A. G. Jones-Williams, who later lost his life in the crash of the first Fairey Long-range Monoplane J9479 on 17 December 1929. (RAF Museum)

63. It is remarkable that, at a time when so much attention was paid to the view from fighter cockpits, the Camel was successful and popular despite the poor outlook it gave its pilot. Here F6240, 'X' of No. 201 Sqn. RAF, exhibits the enlarged centre-section cut-out, introduced on 3 July 1918, that enhanced the pilot's view to the inside of steep turns.

▲ 64

64. One of the outstanding Canadian fighter pilots was Maj. W. G. Barker VC DSO MC**, who won many combat victories in this Clerget Camel, B6313, which he flew from 16 October 1917 to 15 July 1918 with Nos. 28 and 66 Sqns. He took it with him when he assumed command of No. 139 Sqn. RAF, a Bristol F2B unit, on 16 July 1918, and flew it for the last time on 29 September 1918. Here it is seen at Villaverla, not long after Barker took over No. 139 Sqn. (R. C. Shelley)

65. Installations of the 150hp Gnome Monosoupape were tested at Martlesham Heath in B6329 and B2541, probably in anticipation of the standardization of that engine in a batch of Camels for the US Air Service. What Martlesham described as 'the first production machine for USA', properly D6567 (and probably the subject of this photograph), arrived there on (appropriately) 4 July 1918 but had crashed before 20 July. Its replacement, F1336, arrived on 24 July. (MoD)

▼ 65

66. The 110hp Le Rhône engine was preferred by the RFC to the Clerget, and was standardized for night-fighter Camels. Here a standard Camel displays navigation lights on the lower wings, a recognition light above the centre section, and sombre overall finish – all pointers to its nocturnal role. Armament was the standard twin Vickers guns, with Aldis and ring-and-bead sights. (RAF Museum)

67. In the 'Comic' night-fighter conversion first made on B381, the F1/3, the cockpit was moved aft, and two Lewis guns on side-by-side Foster mountings replaced the Vickers guns. The Lewis guns could be either parallel or with the starboard gun at a 45-degree angle. Here B2402 of No. 44 (HD) Sqn. has the former arrangement, with a Neame illuminated sight.

68. After the war ended some F1 and 2F1 Camels fought on in the Russian campaign in 1919. Here Flt. Lt. S. M. Kinkead DSO DSC DFC, commander of 'B' Flight, No. 47 Sqn. RAF, stands beside his Camel, which bears distinctive markings. His Flight was based at Berketovka and received its Camels in September 1919. On 30 September Kinkead shot down a Bolshevik Nieuport that had attacked the DH9s he was escorting. (K. M. Molson)

69. In the postwar period the US Navy had at least six F1 Camels, two with 150hp Gnome Monosoupape engines and four with Clergets. A5721 was one of the latter, and is here seen at Guantanamo with a hydrovane, Grain flotation gear and a large wind-driven generator on the fuselage side. (Fred C. Dickey Jr)

70. The Sopwith TF1 was a modification of an F1 Camel that was made to meet a RFC request of November 1917 for a fighter with downward-firing guns for ground-attack work; the designation signified Trench Fighter. B9278 had underside armour, two downward-firing Lewis guns and a third Lewis on an overwing mounting. It first flew on 15 February 1918, went to France on 7 March, but was not adopted.

71. The 2F1 Camel was a landplane conversion of the FS1, a fighter seaplane design intended to replace the Sopwith Baby. The prototype, N5, went to Martlesham Heath for trials on 15 March 1917, its Lewis gun originally mounted inverted on the centre section. From Martlesham it went to the Isle of Grain, was flying there on 4 April 1917, and was still there in January 1918. When photographed at Grain on 7 June 1917 it had Le Prieur rocket tubes, a generator, a trailing aerial and a revised Lewis-gun installation.

▲72

72. Among the contractors for the production of the 2F1 Camel was William Beardmore & Co. Ltd. N7136, photographed at Dalmuir, underwent its maker's test flights on 4 October 1918 and was delivered to Renfrew that day. The steel-tube centre-section struts and characteristic armament that distinguished the 2F1 can be seen here (RAF Museum)

73. The 2F1 was intended for use at sea and was carried by many capital ships and cruisers on gun-turret flight platforms. Its fuselage, like that of the Schneider/Baby, could be divided aft of the cockpit to save stowage space. Here N6603, flown by Flt. Lt. Tomlinson, takes off from the flying deck of HMS *Pegasus*. This 2F1 was at Grain in early November 1917.

▼73

74. From HMS *Furious* seven 2F1 Camels made the first carrier-borne air strike in history on 19 July 1918 when they bombed the Zeppelin base at Tondern with great success. Some of that historic septet may be in this photograph of *Furious*' flying deck, 15 July 1918.

75. Both F1 and 2F1 Camels were used in experiments in flying off from lighters towed by destroyers, none more hair-raising than that which involved the 2F1 N6623. Its wheels had been replaced by skids like those of the Sopwith 9901a Pup, running in troughs. The take-off attempted by Col. C. R. Samson on 30 May 1918 failed and the pilot was lucky to escape with his life. Here N6623 is seen on lighter *H3* at Felixstowe, 29 May 1918.

74▲　75▼

▲76

▲77 ▼78

76. Spectacular success attended N6812 on 11 August 1918, when Lt. S. D. Culley took off from *H3* and shot down the Zeppelin *L53* off Terschelling. His 2F1 had two overwing Lewis guns. In this photograph, N6812, which retained the normal wheel undercarriage, is aboard the lighter *H3* at Felixstowe. (K. M. Molson)

77. The central figure in the front row is Lt. S. D. Culley; the aircraft is an unusual Sopwith 2F1 armed with twin Vickers guns. It may have been the modified 2F1 that was seen at Felixstowe with a jettisonable undercarriage constructed of unfaired steel tubing.

78. At least eight 2F1s went to the Baltic area in HMS *Vindictive* in 1919 and operated against the Bolsheviks from a rough airstrip at Koivisto. Among these aircraft was N8130 (named 'Tamworth' and thus presumably a presentation aircraft), a Hooper-built 2F1, seen here at Koivisto with another. Both Camels have a bomb in an underfuselage rack; in the background is a Grain Griffin. (RAF Museum)

79. Three of *Vindictive*'s 2F1 Camels were left at Libau late in November 1919 and sent to Riga for Latvian use. These included N8187. All three are seen here at an aviation display held at Riga on 25 July 1920.

80. June 1920: a 2F1 Camel takes off from HMS *Eagle* in a series of deck-flying trials that involved several types of aircraft. An airscrew guard was mounted ahead of the wheels to prevent damage from the fore-and-aft arrester wires of the time; the special catches that engaged these wires can be seen under the spreader bar of the undercarriage.

81. If the Camel restricted its pilot's upward view, the Dolphin went almost to the opposite extreme by placing him in an open centre-section frame, an arrangement that dictated negative stagger on the mainplanes. The first Dolphin prototype, here photographed at Brooklands, had a 200hp Wolseley Adder engine with a deep frontal radiator and high top decking. It underwent initial trials on 22 May 1917 and returned remarkable performance figures.

▲82 ▼83

82. The first prototype Dolphin went to Martlesham Heath for official evaluation early in June 1917, by which time it had been modified slightly. So great was the anxiety to get it to France that its trials were less than thorough. It was flown to France on 13 June by Capt. (later Sir Henry) Tizard, and was flown next day by Capt. W. A. Bishop DSO MC, who reported enthusiastically on it. (T. Heffernan Collection)

83. In the second Dolphin prototype significant modifications were made to improve the pilot's forward and downward view: two inadequate radiators were built into the upper wing roots, the engine cowling was tapered, large cut-outs were made in the lower wings, and a balanced rudder was fitted. This aircraft arrived at Martlesham on 27 July 1917 and returned to Sopwiths on 26 September.

84. The third prototype Dolphin, photographed at Martlesham, where it arrived on 18 October 1917. It had flank-mounted radiators, an enlarged fin, and two Lewis guns on the centre-section frame. On 25 November it went to Orfordness for armament trials, but engine troubles held up its continued testing at Martlesham. After lying engineless for some weeks, it was apparently sent to the Royal Aircraft Factory, Farnborough, in late March 1918.

▲85

85. The fourth prototype Dolphin had a lowered top decking and was essentially the production form of the aircraft. It evidently visited Martlesham Heath, where this photograph was taken. It went to France, was tested at No. 1 Aeroplane Supply Depot (ASD) on 4 November 1917, and went to No. 19 Sqn. RFC on 15 November. Pilots liked it, and it was used operationally, latterly with the serial number B6871. On 26 February 1918 it was recorded as missing. (T. Heffernan Collection)

86. The Dolphin was ordered in very large numbers, but only four operational squadrons were equipped with the type, although further squadrons were in prospect as the war ended. Only one Lewis gun was retained on operational aircraft, such as C3824 of No. 23 Sqn. RFC. This Dolphin was first allocated to the RFC with the Expeditionary Force on 27 December 1917.

87. This Sopwith-built Dolphin, D3775, was the last of 200 (D3576–3775) and was delivered in late May or early June 1918. As aircraft 'N' of No. 87 Sqn. RAF, it was flown by Lt. A. J. Golding. It was one of several aircraft of No. 87 Sqn. that were fitted with a fixed Lewis gun on each lower wing. D3775 survived its operational career and was ferried back to England on 24 January 1919. (RAF Museum)

88. One of the first Sopwith-built production batch of Dolphins was C3854, an aircraft of No. 2 School of Aerial Fighting and Gunnery, Marske. It retained the port Lewis gun on the forward cross-member of the centre-section frame, whereas the official requirement for operational Dolphins in France was the fitting of the starboard Lewis only.

89. The first allocation of a Dolphin to the French government was approved on 27 November 1917. Whether it was fitted with a 300hp Hispano-Suiza is uncertain, but a Dolphin with that engine crashed in France on its first flight late in April 1918. In this photograph D3615 is seen at Villacoublay with the 300hp engine, and was probably the subject of the French official performance report. Production of this version was initiated in France by the SACA (Société Anonyme des Constructions Aéronautiques), and the US Air Service expected to receive 2,194 French-built Dolphins by mid-1919. (Jean Devaux)

▼86

87▲

88▲ 89▼

▲90

90. The 200hp geared Hispano-Suiza was a source of endless trouble, and in 1918 many engines were converted to have direct drive. The first installation of a 'de-geared' engine was made in Dolphin E8914, which arrived at Martlesham on 22 September 1918. Production installations and issues to squadrons followed; the aircraft were designated Dolphin Mk. III, Mk. II having been allotted to the 300hp version. Here C8043 is seen, as aircraft 'Y' of No. 79 Sqn., at Bickendorf in 1919, distinguished by its right-hand airscrew and lowered thrust line.

91. The 7F1 Snipe was originally designed in the summer of 1917 as an undistinguished Camel development clearly intended to give its pilot a better view. When the first prototype, which had a 150hp BR1 engine, appeared at Brooklands it had single-bay wings with little dihedral, a narrow centre section with a small cut-out, a tail unit similar to that of the Camel, a flat-sided fuselage and relatively exposed guns.

▼91

92. In the course of development of the first Snipe prototype the guns were given an extended fairing and the opening in the centre section was enlarged. The dihedral was subsequently increased, as seen in this photograph.
93. Construction of the first Snipe was permitted under official Licence No. 14, but on 31 October 1917 British Requisition No. 224 called for a contract for six prototypes, and the numbers B9962–9967 were allocated on 10 November. The second prototype differed from its predecessor in having a 230hp Bentley BR2: marked B9963, it went to Farnborough on 23 November 1917.

▲94

94. No record of B9964 has yet been found, but this was B9965 as it first appeared, with a fully faired fuselage, a wider centre section, new wing panels, and a revised (but still inadequate) vertical tail with a balanced rudder. From 3 November 1917 Martlesham Heath awaited B9965, but a crash at Brooklands on 19 November delayed its arrival at Martlesham until 18 December. It crashed again on 23 December and was returned to Sopwiths.

95. When B9965 returned to Martlesham on 25 January 1918 it had two-bay wings and, as required by Air Board Type A.1(a) Specification, an overwing Lewis gun. From Martlesham B9965 went to France on 11 March, where it was flown by pilots of Nos. 43 and 65 Sqns. On 1 May it returned to Sopwiths to be fitted with a large spinner; it went back to Martlesham on 27 May for further tests; and it was last reported at Farnborough on 2 July 1918.

96. Effectively the production prototype, B9966 first went to Martlesham, where this photograph was taken, on 18 May 1918, almost two months after production contracts for a total of 1,700 Snipes had been given to seven contractors. B9966 had a slightly enlarged rudder, an adjustable tailplane, and a Badin fuel system. It saw much and varied use as a test aircraft at Martlesham Heath. (Gordon Kinsey)

97. Control response was unsatisfactory, and much of B9966's experimental flying at Martlesham consisted of 'manoeuvrability tests with modified control surfaces' in September and October 1918. It finally had the tail unit seen here, with horn-balanced upper ailerons and wash-out of incidence on the lower starboard aileron. The two-piece triangular tailplane and inversely tapered elevators were considered unsatisfactory and were abandoned. (Gordon Kinsey)

98. Deliveries of production Snipes began at the end of July 1918: by 9 November the Sopwith company had completed delivery of 278, Ruston & Hornsby 20, and Portholme Aerodrome 15. Most of these had the original tail unit and plain upper ailerons, as exemplified by this Snipe, which may have been E8044. When photographed it had a non-standard fuel system and was at Farnborough, where E8044 was recorded in January 1919.

▼95

96 ▲

97 ▲ 98 ▼

99. The initial production form of the Snipe was issued to operational squadrons in France. No. 43 Sqn. RAF was the first to have Snipes, re-equipping on 30 August 1918. One of the fifteen Snipes flown back to Fienvillers from No. 2 ASD on that day was E7989, the third production Snipe built by the Sopwith company, here photographed at Brooklands a matter of days before going to France.

▲100 ▼101

52

102▲

100. One of the war's outstanding aerial actions was fought on this early-production Snipe on 27 October 1918 by Maj. W. G. Barker DSO MC, nominally attached to No. 201 Sqn. Alone he fought at least fifteen German fighters and was wounded in both legs and one arm, but he shot down four of his adversaries and was awarded a richly deserved VC. Here his Snipe, E8102 with his personal markings, is seen after its inevitably heavy landing. Its fuselage is preserved in Canada.

101. This Sopwith photograph of E8184 bears the date 25 November 1918 and depicts the ultimate production form of the Snipe. The upper ailerons are horn-balanced and inversely tapered, whilst the enlarged fin and balanced rudder are generally similar to those evolved on B9966 at Martlesham. The asymmetry of the cockpit's forward coaming can be seen. It seems highly unlikely that any Snipe of this form could have reached France before the Armistice.

102. It was intended to employ the Snipe as a Home Defence fighter, and one aircraft had gone to an HD unit by 31 October 1918. It might have been E8076, the subject of this photograph, which had navigation lights, Holt flare brackets and red-and-blue fuselage roundels and is believed to have gone to No. 78 (HD) Sqn. Eight Snipe Home Defence squadrons were planned for up to April 1919.

▲103

103. Forward planning up to the end of April 1919 also provided for five Snipe squadrons with the anti-submarine forces, which is doubtless why E8068 was at Grain in mid-October 1918 in the form seen here. The undercarriage wheels could be jettisoned, and a hydro-vane was mounted ahead of the undercarriage, both measures to minimize the risk of overturning on ditching.

104. The 7F1a Snipe Mk. Ia had greatly increased tank-age to enable it to act as an escort fighter to bombers of the Independent Force. The prototype installation was made in E8089, and fifty production aircraft were manufactured; several were issued to squadrons after the Armistice, despite the variant's structural inadequacies. E8242 was a Snipe Ia, identified by the circular access hole for the main tank filler, just behind the cockpit on the port side. (Chaz Bowyer)

105. The Snipe remained in service with several RAF fighter squadrons for some years after the Armistice. In this photograph a Snipe of No. 1 Sqn. is seen in the heat of Iraq, in overall aluminium finish and with a rack for small bombs under the fuselage. The fuel system has been modified, the venturi tube of the Badin system having been replaced by a Rotherham pump.

▲104 ▼105

106. Great things were expected of the 320hp ABC Dragonfly radial engine, and many British aircraft types of 1918 were designed around it. The final Snipe prototype, B9967, was fitted with a Dragonfly and had a lengthened fuselage while retaining the early small fin and rudder. It arrived at Farnborough on 11 May 1918, where it was much used in the unavailing struggle to make the Dragonfly perform safely and satisfactorily.

107. The Dragonfly-powered Snipe, first designated Snipe Mk.II, was put into production with the name 'Dragon' at the end of October 1918. E7990 was the production prototype, having the final Snipe fin and rudder but retaining plain upper ailerons. It appeared in January 1919 and went to Martlesham on 14 February. It seemed to spend most of its time on the ground and was eventually returned to Sopwiths by rail on 7 July 1919.

108. Thirty Snipes, F7001–7030, ordered under a contract originally dated 3 May 1918, were built as Dragons. Deliveries started in June 1919 and were completed next month, running parallel with deliveries from the larger batch of Dragons, J3617–3916. These all had balanced upper ailerons and steel-tube centre-section struts. F7017 is seen here at Martlesham, where it arrived on 12 November 1919. It flew for a time with a modified Dragonfly from Nighthawk J2403. (MoD)

106▲

107▲ 108▼

▲109

▲110 ▼111

109. Doubtless inspired by the armouring of the TF1, the Sopwith design office created the TF2 Salamander, in which the forward fuselage was constructed of armour plate. The first of three prototypes, E5429, is here pictured at Brooklands, 1 May 1918, having been taken aloft for its maiden flight on 27 April. It went to France on 9 May, visiting Nos. 3, 73 and 65 Sqns., but it crashed on 19 May, was struck off at No. 2 ASD on 29 May, and probably never returned to England.

110. As the Salamander was intended to be a low-flying ground-attack fighter it was a suitable subject for the camouflage scheme devised at Orfordness. The third prototype, E5431, which had arrived at Martlesham on 24 June 1918 for trials, was painted as seen here and sent to France late in July for evaluation. Unfortunately it crashed before this was undertaken. (*Aeromodeller*)

111. Despite many similarities to the Snipe, the Salamander differed substantially in its structure and there was little interchangeability between the two. Early production Salamanders had, like early Snipes, small fins and plain upper ailerons as seen here on F6504, a production Salamander that, as early as 22 October 1918, was with No. 157 Sqn., one of the first units to mobilize with the type. (R. N. Benwell)

112. The Salamander's control problems were similar to those of the Snipe, and later production aircraft had balanced upper ailerons and the large fin-and-rudder resembling, but structurally stronger than, their Snipe counterparts. Here F6602 exemplifies the final production Salamander.

113. A batch of 150 Salamanders was ordered from the Air Navigation Co. Ltd. Twenty were cancelled on 20 December 1918; 107 had been delivered by 5 July 1919; and the balance of the order was also cancelled. Here the first ANC-built Salamander, F7801, displays its camouflage at Brooklands. By mid-August 1919, Sopwiths had delivered 334 Salamanders; Glendower, Palladium Autocars and Wolseley contributed 85, to make a total of 526 known deliveries. (RAF Museum)

114. The Sopwith 3F2 Hippo (200hp Clerget 11Eb) was designed about April 1917 as a two-seat fighter, primarily with French orders in view; heavy negative stagger was adopted to give the pilot a clear outlook. Initially balanced ailerons and a very small fin were fitted, and there was 3° of dihedral. The Hippo first flew on 13 September 1917 but engine problems delayed until 29 December its arrival – with the recorded identity of X11 – at Martlesham, the locale for this photograph. (E. F. Cheeseman)

112▲

113▲ 114▼

▲115

115. Having had a lukewarm report from Martlesham, the Hippo returned to Sopwiths on 2 February 1918 for overhaul and the transfer of its engine to the first Bulldog. Perhaps the company still hoped for French orders, since the aircraft was fitted with new wings, plain ailerons and an enlarged fin, although it retained its pillar gun-mountings in the rear cockpit for a time. In this modified form the Hippo was photographed at Brooklands. (RAF Museum)

116. By early April 1918 the Hippo's dihedral had been increased to 5°, but stagger was reduced, a Scarff ring mounting was fitted to the rear cockpit, and its serial number belatedly was painted on. New steel-tube 'V'-struts replaced the earlier wooden members in the undercarriage. What appeared to be a second Hippo, X18, was reported in June 1918.

117. The Sopwith 2FR2 Bulldog was a fighter-reconnaissance two-seater with the 200hp Clerget 11E. It first appeared as seen here at Brooklands, with single-bay wings and pillar-mounted Lewis guns for the observer, and flew late in 1917.

▲116 ▼117

118. In an attempt to improve the Bulldog's unsatisfactory handling qualities, the aircraft was fitted with two-bay wings having balanced ailerons. Maker's trials of the modified aircraft occupied March and much of April 1918 and apparently led to the abandonment of the balanced ailerons: new wings with plain ailerons were fitted, but no effort was made to replace the impractical gun mountings in the rear cockpit.

119. Marked 'X3' and fitted with its new two-bay wings with plain ailerons, the Bulldog went to Martlesham on 22 April 1918. It now handled well but its performance disappointed, and it had been damaged by 11 May. Repaired, it was at Orfordness by 12 June 1918, and the aircraft was extensively used there on experimental work. By 12 October its Clerget had been replaced by a BR2, and it finally flew to Hendon on 2 September 1919.

120. The second Bulldog, X4, was completed with a 320hp ABC Dragonfly radial for use as a test-bed for that incurably troublesome engine. It went to the Royal Aircraft Establishment at Farnborough on 25 June 1918 and was much used in the extensive but (as it proved) futile attempts to resolve the Dragonfly's problems. These included a change to a Dragonfly Mk.II early in 1919, and X4 was still at Farnborough in March 1919.

118▲

119▲ 120▼

▲121

121. On 24 November 1917 an order for four Sopwith single-seat fighters with the 170hp ABC Wasp radial was requested, and on 10 December the number was increased to six; the first four were to be of conventional construction, the others to have a monocoque fuselage. The name 'Snail' was approved on 16 February 1918. Only C4284 was built with the fabric-covered fuselage, and this aeroplane had slight negative stagger. It was sent to Brooklands on 4 April 1918 and apparently went to Martlesham on 9 May. It survived until November 1919, but by then had decayed irremediably.

122. Although some work was done on C4285 and C4286, only C4288 was built with the monocoque fuselage and positive stagger. It is uncertain whether C4284 was actually tested at Martlesham, but C4288 undoubtedly was, and this photograph was taken there. The monocoque Snail proved to be disappointing, and the design was finally abandoned in October 1918 when it was decided not to produce the ABC Wasp engine. Like C4284, C4288 was to decay until November 1919.

▼122

123. The use of a monoplane conversion of the Camel as a shipboard fighter was discussed at an official conference on 23 August 1918, and the aircraft appeared in mid-October, having been named 'Swallow' by 4 September. Essentially it was an F1 Camel fuselage, that of B9276, with modified gun installation and a parasol wing and powered by a 110hp Le Rhône. This photograph was taken at Brooklands in October 1918.

124. On 29 October 1918 the Swallow went to Martlesham, where this photograph was taken, for official trials. These were apparently conducted at a leisurely pace, for the aircraft remained at Martlesham until May 1919. It was decided on 17 May that nothing further was to be done with the Swallow. (MoD)

▲125 ▼126

125. In addition to the Dragon, Sopwith designed two new fighters for the Dragonfly radial engine. The contract for three Snark triplane prototypes was dated 14 May 1918. F4068 was the first of the three and, in addition to the two fixed Vickers, could have four Lewis guns under the bottom wings. All three Snarks had a plywood monocoque fuselage.

126. Here the third Snark, F4070, is seen at Martlesham, where all three aircraft were tested; it had a more refined engine installation with a large spinner. F4068 arrived at Martlesham on 12 November 1919, F4069 on 17 March 1920, and F4070 was there in December 1920. Apart from engine problems, the fuselages deteriorated: that of F4069 was unserviceable by 17 July 1920, and that of F4070 was so strained by 24 May 1921 that authority to write it off was requested.

127. The last Sopwith single-seat fighter design was the Snapper, the contract under which three prototypes, F7031–7033, were ordered being dated 6 June 1918. An early intention to use a monocoque fuselage was abandoned in favour of conventional structure, and F7031 was complete and awaiting its engine by 18 September 1918. Its maker's trials were apparently flown in the latter half of July 1919.

128. Snapper F7031 arrived at Martlesham for official trials on 1 August 1919, fitted with a large spinner and modified engine cowling. Trials were conducted spasmodically, owing to engine problems and flying-wire breakages, until 25 October 1919: a speed of 138mph at 10,000ft and a climb to that altitude in 7min 47sec were recorded. Alterations to the wings were called for. All three Snappers were reported at Farnborough in June 1920. (MoD)

▲129

▲130 ▼131

129. Initially at least, Sopwiths regarded the Buffalo two-seater as a trench fighter; officially it was a contact-patrol aircraft, its armoured fuselage derived structurally from the Salamander, and two were built. It was briefly known as the Armoured Bulldog and incorporated some Bulldog components. H5892 was at Brooklands on 18 September 1918 and flew to France on 27 September. It went to No. 4 Sqn. Australian Flying Corps on 9 October, returned to No. 1 ASD on 20 October and moved back to England on 26 October.

130. H5892 went to Europe again in 1919, having been allocated to the RAF there on 29 April. It had been fitted with a Scarff ring mounting to replace the pillar mounting originally provided for the observer's Lewis gun. With H5893, it went to No. 43 Sqn. at Bickendorf, where this photograph was taken.

131. H5893 had a Scarff No. 2 ring mounting from the outset, an enlarged rudder, and extended armour. It arrived at Martlesham for trials on 18 November 1918 and stayed at least until 10 May 1919. Like H5892, it was assigned to the Expeditionary Force on 29 April, but it crashed on a landing approach in Germany. Both aircraft had the 230hp Bentley BR2 rotary engine, but performance was undistinguished, and the Buffalo might have fared badly in air-to-air combat.